THE OFFIC[IAL]
QUEENS [PARK]
RANGERS
ANNUAL 2019

THIS BOOK BELONGS TO...

Name:	Age:
Favourite Player:	

MY 2018/19 PREDICTIONS...	ACTUAL...
QPR's Final Position:	
QPR's Top Scorer:	
Sky Bet Championship League Champions:	
Sky Bet Championship Top Scorer:	
Emirates FA Cup Winners:	
Carabao Cup Winners:	
Teams to be relegated: 22nd	
23rd	
24th	

g

A Grange Publication

Written by Francis Atkinson and Matt Webb
Designed by Paul Galbraith and John Anderson

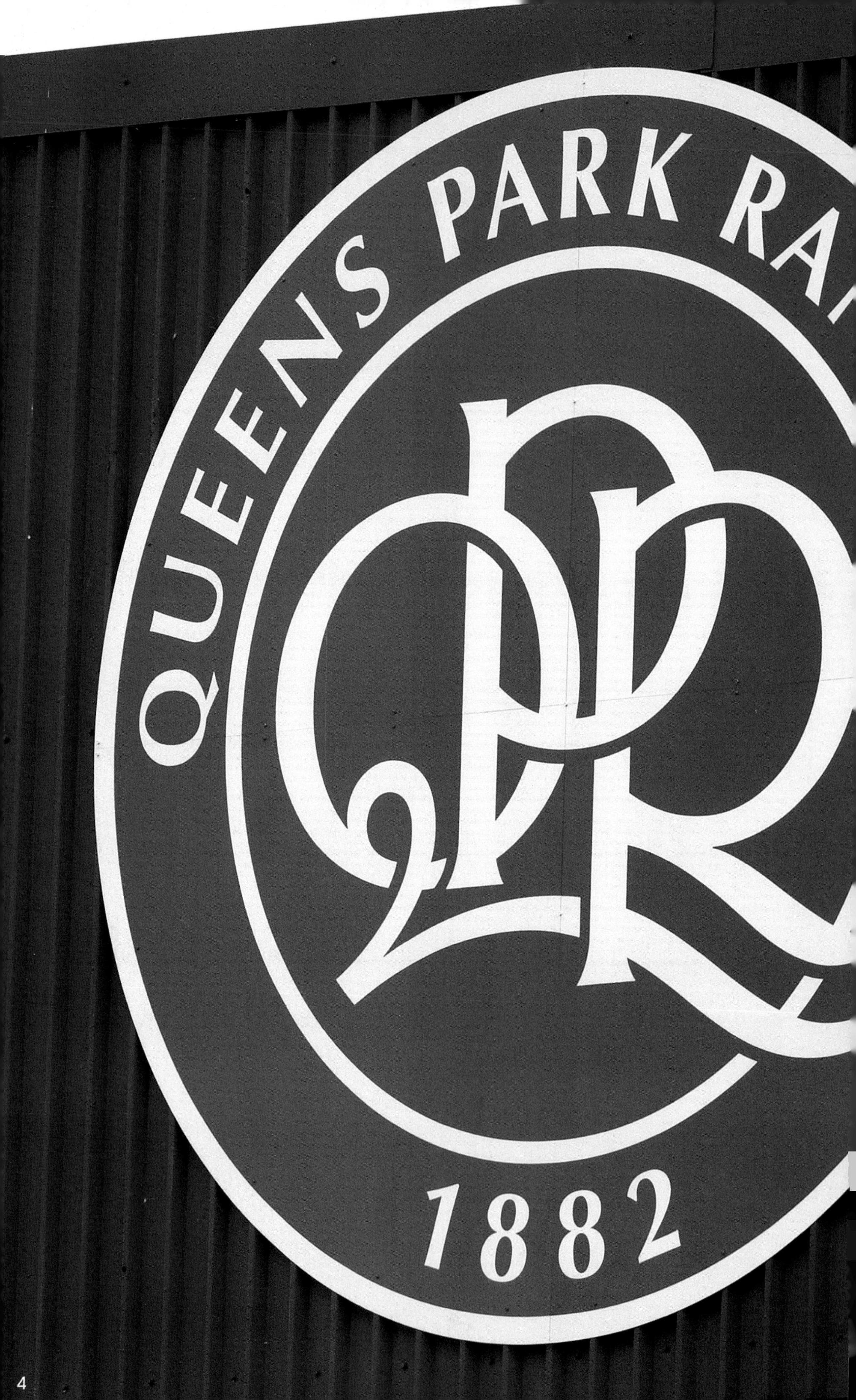
QUEENS PARK
1882

CONTENTS

PRETTY IN PINK!

QPR's new kits for the 2018/19 season were unveiled in late June – created through a collaborative creative process between the club and our kit supplier, Errea.

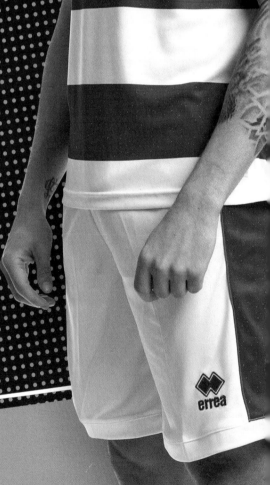

The home shirt could be described as a 'classic with a twist'. It has the broad blue and white hoops that R's fans expect but with an added touch of colour, with the red sleeve piping and three-colour collar and cuffs.

In addition, the royal blue hoops contain a tonal pinstripe effect which is as subtle as it is effective.

Combine all that with Errea's renowned mundial fabric and you have a shirt for Rangers fans to be proud of.

The away shirt reflects the design of the home but in fuchsia pink, with the famous hoops being created by groups of darker pink stripes.

NEW KITS
2018/19

The tricolour trims have once again been added, which give both shirts a retro feel and, as with the home shirt, the detailing on the inside of the collar adds an extra level of quality to an already perfectly-tailored shirt.

R's boss Steve McClaren said: "The QPR home kit is so iconic in English football. It's a very recognisable and famous strip, and it has a real tradition about it.

"I really like the kits for this season, home and away.

"My job and the job of my staff and players is to do all we can to make sure that these are successful kits. That's what we will be putting all our efforts into."

Fabrizio Taddei, head of Errea's pro clubs department, added: "We truly hope the fans will appreciate these new kits, the work and attention to detail that has gone into them, and will enjoy wearing them next season as much as we have enjoyed producing them."

FAITH IN

RANGERS BETTERED BOTH THEIR POINTS TALLY AND LEAGUE POSITION FROM THE PREVIOUS CAMPAIGN IN 2017/18.

But arguably the biggest positive to come from last season was the emergence of a number of the club's young stars.

There were league debuts for the likes of Ilias Chair, Ebere Eze, Osman Kakay, Bright Osayi-Samuel, Aramide Oteh and Paul Smyth.

And in QPR's final home fixture of the campaign – a 3-1 win against Birmingham City at Loftus Road – the average age of the team was just 23 years and 16 days old.

Just like our new away strip, the future's seemingly bright!

EBERE EZE

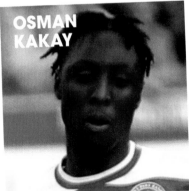

OSMAN KAKAY

PAUL SMYTH

YOUTH!

ARAMIDE OTEH

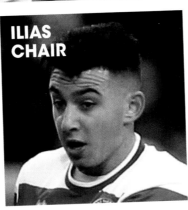

ILIAS CHAIR

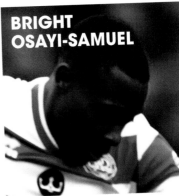

BRIGHT OSAYI-SAMUEL

IN NUMBERS

Looking at the key stats from QPR's 2017/18 Sky Bet Championship campaign...

POINTS WON:

56

WINS

15

DRAWS

11

XXXXX
XXXXX
XXXXX
XXXXX

LOSSES: 20

GOALS SCORED:

58

MOST ASSISTS

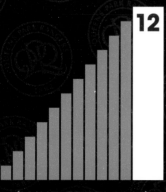

12

(LUKE FREEMAN)

TOP GOALSCORER:

11

(MATT SMITH)

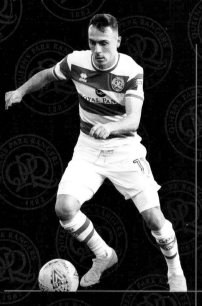

MOST SUCCESSFUL PASSES:

1,534
(JOSH SCOWEN)

MOST SUCCESSFUL DRIBBLES:

135
(MATT SMITH)

AVG. POSSESSION:
50.3%

MOST APPEARANCES:

46
JAKE BIDWELL

GOALS CONCEDED:

70

CLEAN SHEETS:

7

MOST TACKLES WON:

149
(MASSIMO LUONGO)

MOST AERIAL DULES WON:

284
(MATT SMITH)

YELLOW CARDS:

84

RED CARDS:

5

YOU ARE

1 At the start of a local derby match at the coin toss, the two captains (who are bitter rivals) refuse to shake hands and instead start trading insults. It then becomes heated very quickly and punches are exchanged. What action do you take?

2 In the final moments of a match the ball is punted out for a throw-in but before it fully crosses the touchline the home manager, who is standing right by the field of play, steps forward to catch the ball. He tosses it to his player to take a quick throw but the manager's foot has already crossed onto the pitch as he caught the ball. Now what?

3 It is injury time and a player goes down near the touchline apparently injured, with his team winning 1-0. The opposing captain is fed up with the continued time wasting and reacts by carrying him off the pitch against his will, with the injured player's physio now screaming abuse at the captain too. How do you handle it?

4 As a player commits a terrible red card tackle he also suffers himself by picking up a really bad injury. A mass player brawl follows and as you are trying to control things the injured player, who committed the offence, is taken off in agony before you had a chance to show him the red card. Your fourth official has let a substitute come on in his place. Is this ok?

THE REF

5 A home team is defending a slim lead in the closing stages of a match by playing the ball across their backline. You check your watch and decide to blow for full time but as you raise the whistle you drop it in the mud. As you bend down to get it the opposing striker has nipped in to steal the ball and drive a fierce long-range shot into the net. They have equalised, or have they? What happens?

6 A defender makes a last-ditch clearance which flies off towards the corner flag, knocking it clean out of its hole. It's impossible to see whether it was a corner or a throw-in and your linesman also can't tell. So what do you decide?

ANSWERS

1 The easy part is to firstly send both players off. Then adjust the line-ups as the game hadn't started therefore both managers can change a sub into a starting player. This means both teams will start with 11 players each but will only have six players each to use as substitutes. Both teams can still make three changes during the course of the match.

2 Stop the throw-in and have a strong word with the manager for stepping onto the field of play. You then restart with a dropped ball from where the manager stepped onto the pitch.

3 You first need to caution the captain or even give him a red card if he has used excessive force in removing the injured opponent. Then make sure the injured player is okay, calming down the physio at the same time. Make it clear to all concerned that time wasting will be firmly dealt with.

4 Firstly your fourth official has put you in a difficult position, they have no authority to sanction a substitution and you tell them so firmly. Secondly play hasn't restarted so ask the substitute to leave the field of play and make an announcement that the injured player has been shown a red card.

5 Timekeeping is solely down to you and you had decided that time was up before the interception and goal. You won't be popular with the visitors but everyone will have seen you drop your whistle as you were about to blow so you need to disallow the goal and explain why. A sensible precaution would be to attach the whistle to a lanyard and wrap it around your wrist.

6 You can award a dropped ball close to the corner but you would ideally give a corner or throw-in to the attacking team as the ball went out of play. Preferably a throw as the corner would favour the attacking team more. On balance a throw-in is the fairest option.

PAWEL
WSZOLEK

14

EBERE EZE

15

DOUBLE

WITH two hairstyles that wouldn't have looked out of place in a Status Quo line-up, **Gary Bannister** and **John Byrne** really did strike up a dynamic frontline partnership at Loftus Road.

Bannister was a lethal poacher with that natural goalscorer's instinct – Byrne possessed plenty of flair and wore our famous number 10 shirt with tremendous style and swagger.

Sporting the classic QPR Guinness kits as well as their rock-star locks, the duo were particularly good on our former plastic pitch together – Bannister's crowning moment in Rangers colours coming on Easter Monday, 1986 when he scored a hat-trick in our 6-0 win over Chelsea. Byrne, who also chipped in with his fair share of goals, was on the scoresheet twice that day.

GARY BANNISTER

BORN in Warrington, Cheshire, Bannister made 22 appearances for Coventry City before switching to Sheffield Wednesday for £100,000 in 1981.

Gary made an instant impact at Hillsborough, notching 22 goals in his first season in the Steel City, and 66 in all.

QPR came calling for his services in 1984, paying £200,000 to secure the striker, and he scored 72 goals over 172 appearances in a successful spell at Loftus Road. Bannister returned to Coventry in 1988.

Gary was signed by former R's boss Alan Mullery. He was a diminutive, quick and intelligent centre-forward who was quick to punish mistakes made by opposition defenders.

TROUBLE

JOHN BYRNE

ORIGINATING from Manchester, John was spotted playing in a local park by a taxi driver – who in turn recommended the forward to York City.

Byrne was a naturally-gifted footballer with impressive close ball control. He was also an international with the Republic of Ireland, who won the first of his 23 senior caps while with the R's.

John went on to become a huge success at Sunderland, scoring in every round of the 1992 FA Cup from the third round, bar the final.

In all, he registered 36 goals for Rangers over 149 outings.

STEVE McCLAREN
IN PROFILE

QPR appointed Steve McClaren as our new manager in May, to replace the outgoing Ian Holloway at the Loftus Road helm.

Here's a detailed look at the 57-year-old's career in football...

Steve McClaren joined QPR having amassed a wealth of experience throughout his 23 years of coaching.

McClaren, who was born in York, spent the bulk of his playing career at Hull City, for whom he made 178 appearances and scored 16 goals. The ex-midfielder also had other spells with Derby County, Lincoln City, Oxford United and Bristol City, before hanging his boots up in 1992 because of injury.

Having always had a desire to coach, McClaren's first foray into management was at Oxford, where he oversaw the youth and reserve teams.

In 1995, he was offered the opportunity to return to Derby as the assistant manager to Jim Smith. The pair proved to be very successful together, winning promotion to the Premier League at the first time of asking and stabilising the Rams in the top division.

McClaren's name was beginning to grow within the management world, and he was establishing himself as a master tactician and effectively the brains behind Derby's success.

In early 1999, when Brian Kidd left Manchester United, Sir Alex Ferguson was determined to make McClaren his assistant and landed his man shortly after Kidd's departure.

McClaren became an instant success at United, helping them to an unmatched domestic and European treble, where the Red Devils won the Premier League title, FA Cup and UEFA Champions League.

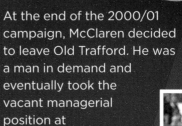

At the end of the 2000/01 campaign, McClaren decided to leave Old Trafford. He was a man in demand and eventually took the vacant managerial position at Middlesbrough.

In his first season, McClaren took the Teessiders to an improved 12th-place finish in the top-flight, while also guiding them to the FA Cup semi-finals. They were narrowly defeated by eventual-winners Arsenal.

SM
errea

His next season ended with another respectable league finish, but it was in 2003/04 when McClaren's quality as a coach really shone through. He guided Boro to their first-ever major domestic trophy – defeating Bolton Wanderers to win the League Cup.

Middlesbrough were able to attract some big names to the Riverside that summer, with European football guaranteed through their cup victory. And Boro went on to have an excellent campaign, finishing in seventh position.

The following season turned out to be McClaren's final year with Boro. Remarkably, they managed to make the UEFA Cup final, producing some excellent comebacks along the way, but were defeated 4-0 in the final by Sevilla.

In 2006, after the World Cup, the England national team were looking for a replacement for Sven-Goran Eriksson. McClaren had been involved with previous England squads, and that combined with the success he had at Middlesbrough made him the leading candidate for the job.

He was selected as Three Lions manager on a four-year deal. However, despite winning his first two games in charge, his spell with England lasted less than 16 months.

Looking for a new challenge, McClaren opted to go abroad and was appointed as head coach of FC Twente in June 2008.

He enjoyed a wonderful spell with the Dutch outfit, winning the league in his second season – and becoming the first Englishman to manage a team to a top-level domestic league title since Bobby Robson with FC Porto in 1996. McClaren was unsurprisingly named manager of the year.

In 2010, he left Twente to become the first Englishman to manage in the Bundesliga after accepting a job at Wolfsburg. His time with the German side was short lived, as six months later he was relieved of his duties.

McClaren then had a spell with Nottingham Forest before returning to Twente. A role as part of the coaching staff at QPR followed for three months while, in September 2013, he was appointed the manager of Derby.

He impressively guided the Rams to a third-place finish in the Championship, and with it a spot in the end-of-season play-offs. But McClaren could not mastermind a win against the team he began the start of the campaign with – Rangers victorious at Wembley thanks to a late Bobby Zamora winner.

The following season, Derby were on course to reach the play-offs again but narrowly missed out because of defeat on the final day to Reading. McClaren left the Rams and joined Premier League side Newcastle, for whom he was the manager of for just short of nine months.

McClaren later returned to Pride Park, but could not reach the heights of his previous two seasons and left only six months into the job. Most recently he had been working as a coaching consultant with Israeli club Maccabi Tel Aviv, a role he left at the end of 2017.

McClaren became QPR manager on May 18th 2018 – signing a two-year contract at Loftus Road.

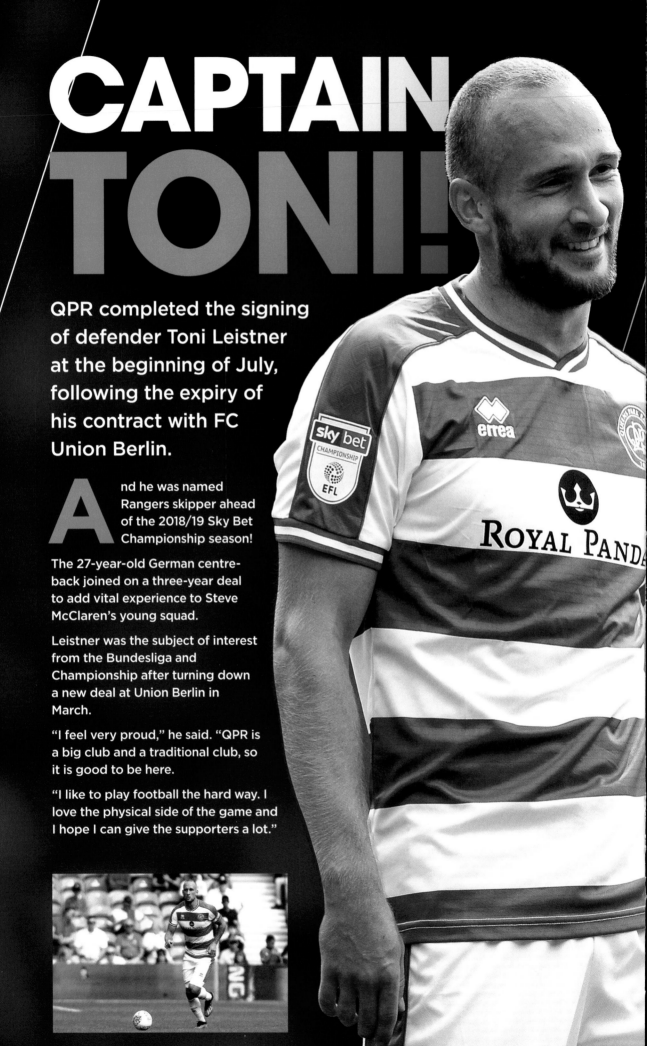

CAPTAIN TONI!

QPR completed the signing of defender Toni Leistner at the beginning of July, following the expiry of his contract with FC Union Berlin.

And he was named Rangers skipper ahead of the 2018/19 Sky Bet Championship season!

The 27-year-old German centre-back joined on a three-year deal to add vital experience to Steve McClaren's young squad.

Leistner was the subject of interest from the Bundesliga and Championship after turning down a new deal at Union Berlin in March.

"I feel very proud," he said. "QPR is a big club and a traditional club, so it is good to be here.

"I like to play football the hard way. I love the physical side of the game and I hope I can give the supporters a lot."

A close friend of Seb Polter, Leistner admits he sought the opinion of the former R's striker who encouraged him to make the move to Loftus Road.

"He told me only good things about QPR." Leistner added. "He said the fans are very crazy, positive and he loved playing here.

"I also met the manager and he convinced me with the style he wants to play. It made my choice easy."

"HE IS A LEADER, A WINNER AND DOMINANT IN THE AIR"

Leistner became McClaren's first signing as QPR boss, and the R's chief was delighted with his capture.

"With Nedum Onuoha, Jack Robinson and James Perch leaving the club, and Grant Hall coming back from a long-term injury, we are obviously short in that area," McClaren said.

"We have been looking for the last month for centre-backs, and we believe we have found a very good one in Toni.

"He has been much sought after, he's run his contract down and many people were chasing his signature, from the Bundesliga and the Championship.

"I have watched him play, we have done a lot of character references on him and I went out to Berlin to meet him, to look him in the eye and speak with him.

"He is a leader, a winner and dominant in the air but can also play, so he seems an ideal fit for how we want to go forward.

"We have got a young squad, and Onuoha, Robinson and Perch were all experienced players, so getting someone in of Toni's age and experience is crucial.

"I am delighted to have got him."

FACTFILE

NAME
TONI LEISTNER

....

DATE OF BIRTH
AUGUST 19TH 1990

....

COUNTRY
GERMANY

....

PREVIOUS CLUBS
SC BOREA, DYNAMO DRESDEN, HALLESCHER (LOAN), UNION BERLIN

CHAMPIONS TOPPLED

QPR overcame eventual runaway Sky Bet Championship winners Wolves 2-1 at Loftus Road last October, in what was arguably our finest home victory of the 2017/18 campaign.

Matt Smith's 81st-minute header secured all three points, after Wanderers' Leo Bonatini (43 minutes) had earlier cancelled out Conor Washington's opening goal in the 41st minute.

QPR A to Z

Our alphabetical look at all things Rangers...

A IS FOR...

Allen. Family members Bradley, Clive, Martin and Les have all played for the Super Hoops.

B IS FOR...

Bowles. 'Stan The Man' – arguably our greatest-ever player.

C IS FOR...

Currie. Tony skippered the R's during our 1982 FA Cup final replay against Tottenham Hotspur.

D IS FOR...

Day. Goalkeeper Chris is well-liked by Rangers fans for his spell in W12 just after the turn of the century.

E IS FOR...

England captain. Midfield man Gerry Francis proudly led both QPR and his country as a player.

F IS FOR...

Ferdinand. 'Sir Les' – our current director of football – was a sharpshooter for the R's in the nineties.

G IS FOR...

Goddard. George is QPR's record league goalscorer (172).

H IS FOR...

Hill. Clint's never-say-die attitude won the hearts of R's fans between 2010-16.

I IS FOR...

Ingham. Former player Tony is our highest league appearance maker (519).

J IS FOR...

Jude the Cat – Rangers' friendly feline mascot!

K IS FOR...

Keen. Skipper Mike lifted the League Cup for QPR in 1967.

L IS FOR...

L

M IS FOR...

M

N IS FOR...

N

O IS FOR...

Loftus Road – our famous home (barring the odd move away) since 1917.

Marsh. Like Stan Bowles, Rodney is another iconic former R's number 10.

Nine-two – our all-time record win for goals scored (v Tranmere Rovers (H), Division Three, 03/12/1960).

P IS FOR...

P

Q IS FOR...

Q

R IS FOR...

R

Pigbag. 'Der, der, der, der, HOOPS!'

Queens Park Rangers. Our name since Christchurch Rangers and St. Jude's Institute came together in 1886.

Rowlands. Martin enjoyed promotion with the R's in 2003/04, and went on to captain us.

Ollie. Ian Holloway's contribution to the club as both a player and manager will never be forgotten.

S IS FOR...

S

T IS FOR...

T

U IS FOR...

U

V IS FOR...

V

Stock. Alec is QPR's greatest-ever boss.

Taarabt. Moroccan magician Adel was a big reason why Rangers won promotion to the Premier League in 2010/11.

Ulsterman. Ex-Northern Ireland defender Alan McDonald is our most-capped player (52).

Venables. Former player and boss 'El Tel' led us to the FA Cup final in 1982 – as well as the top-flight a year later.

W IS FOR...

W

X IS FOR...

X

Y IS FOR...

Y

Z IS FOR...

WXY

White City. The closest tube stop to Loftus Road Stadium.

X-Factor. Bowles, Byrne, Marsh, Taarabt and Wegerle – the list goes on.

Youngest-ever player – Frank Sibley (15 years & 275 days old).

Zamoraaaaaaa! Bobby Zamora – our 2014 Championship play-off final hero.

RAY WILKINS

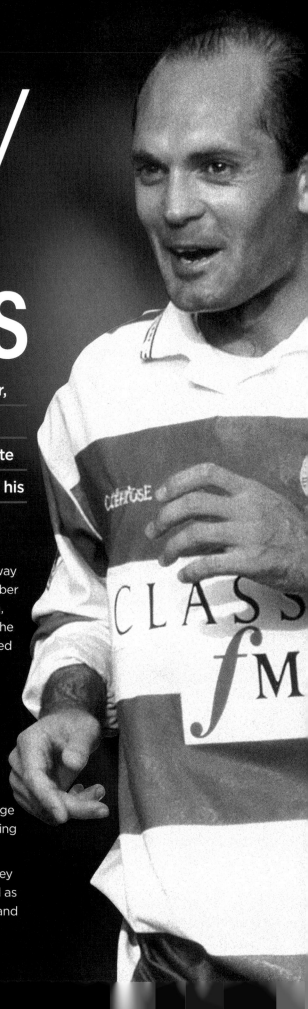

A BRILLIANT passing midfielder, Ray Wilkins made over 200 appearances for Rangers – despite joining us during the later years of his playing career.

R ay, of course, sadly passed away in April 2018. Born on September 14th 1956 in nearby Hillingdon, Middlesex, he came through the ranks at Chelsea, and captained their first team at only 18.

Wilkins subsequently starred for Manchester United, AC Milan, Paris Saint-Germain and Glasgow Rangers, winning 84 England caps.

'Butch' moved from Ibrox – the home of Scottish giants Rangers – to QPR on a free transfer in December 1989. Many pundits thought that Wilkins was over the hill at the age of 33, but he went on to dispel such talk following 207 appearances and 10 goals for the R's.

Ray was outstanding for Rangers, playing a key role in our success in the early 1990s – as well as the emergence of players such as Les Ferdinand and Andy Sinton.

His form was so good, in fact, that there was even talk of an England recall.

After moving away for a short spell at Crystal Palace, Wilkins returned to Loftus Road as our player-manager in November 1994.

Rangers finished eighth in the Premier League that season, but star striker Ferdinand was sold to Newcastle United for £6million in the summer and that led to relegation in 1995/96.

Ray remained in charge for the first month of the following season, before leaving again in September 1996.

HE SET A RECORD AS QPR'S OLDEST-EVER OUTFIELD PLAYER

He set a record as QPR's oldest-ever outfield player when appearing versus Bolton Wanderers on September 1st 1996, at the age of 39 years and 352 days old.

Short playing spells followed at Wycombe Wanderers, Hibernian, Millwall and Leyton Orient, before Wilkins hung up his boots and became manager of Fulham.

He later had a spell on the coaching staff at Chelsea, and worked as a football pundit on TV and radio.

Ray, who received an MBE in 1993 for his services to sport, was inducted into The Forever R's Club – our ex-players' association – in October 2016.

ALL CHANGE!

The Sky Bet Championship has six new runners and riders for the 2018/19 season. Here's a lowdown on those who have joined us for the current campaign...

PREMIER PROFILE

STAR MAN
Ryan Shawcross (CB)

STOKE CITY

Manager: Gary Rowett
Nickname: The Potters
Ground: bet365 Stadium
Capacity: 30,089
Distance From W12: 161.4 miles
(2 hrs 39 mins)
2017/18 Position: 19th
(Premier League)

With all three newly-promoted teams avoiding the Premier League's trap door come the end of last season, it was left to some more established top-flight clubs to slip to relegation. Stoke won promotion to the big league back in 2008 but could never recover from a poor start under Mark Hughes in 2017/18 – despite swapping Hughes for Paul Lambert in January. Former Derby County, Birmingham City and Burton Albion boss Gary Rowett is now at the helm in the Potteries, as Stoke search for an instant return.

SWANSEA CITY

Manager: Graham Potter
Nickname: The Swans
Ground: Liberty Stadium
Capacity: 21,088
Distance From W12: 186.2 miles
(3 hrs 18 mins)
2017/18 Position: 18th
(Premier League)

After replacing Paul Clement in the Liberty hotseat last December, Carlos Carvalhal looked to have steered City to safety in 2017/18 – only for a late wobble seeing the Swans relegated to the Championship. Swansea – who include former QPR attacking midfielder Leroy Fer in their ranks – have since appointed English coach Graham Potter as their manager, following his success in Sweden with Ostersund. This is City's first season at this level since they were promoted to the Premier League alongside the R's in 2010/11. A repeat of that would certainly be welcomed in west London!

STAR MAN
Barrie McKay (AM)

WEST BROMWICH ALBION

STAR MAN
Matt Phillips (AM)

Manager: Darren Moore
Nickname: The Baggies
Ground: The Hawthorns
Capacity: 26,688
Distance From W12: 125.0 miles
(2 hrs 6 mins)
2017/18 Position: 20th
(Premier League)

After replacing Alan Pardew in the managerial hotseat towards the end of last season, Baggies legend Darren Moore couldn't quite guide West Brom to a great escape from relegation. However, his efforts in caretaker charge were enough to land him the top job on a permanent basis. Since the turn of the century, West Brom have yo-yoed between the Premier League and Championship – and will be hoping to book a swift return to England's top division under cult hero Moore.

ON THE UP

BLACKBURN ROVERS

Manager: Tony Mowbray
Nickname: Rovers
Ground: Ewood Park
Capacity: 31,367
Distance From W12: 228.2 miles
(3 hrs 49 mins)
2017/18 Position: 2nd
(League One)

Tony Mowbray and his Blackburn team are back at this level after pushing Wigan all the way for the League One title last term. Rovers eased to an immediate return to the Championship in the end, with their impressive tally of 96 points seeing them finish some nine above third-placed Shrewsbury Town. The former Premier League champions were last in the top division six years ago, and will be hoping to continue their current ascent in 2018/19.

STAR MAN
Bradley Dack (AM)

ROTHERHAM UNITED

STAR MAN
Will Vaulks (CM)

Manager: Paul Warne
Nickname: The Millers
Ground: AESSEAL New York Stadium
Capacity: 12,021
Distance From W12: 163.6 miles
(2 hrs 53 mins)
2017/18 Position: 4th (League One, promoted via play-offs)

The Millers held their nerve during extra-time at Wembley in late May to secure a 2-1 League One play-off final win over Shrewsbury Town. Victory meant that United were back in England's second tier just 13 months after their relegation in 2016/17. Boss Paul Warne – who signed a new three-year deal in June – will be hoping that Rotherham can use lessons learned from their last visit to the Championship to their advantage.

WIGAN ATHLETIC

Manager: Paul Cook
Nickname: The Latics
Ground: DW Stadium
Capacity: 25,133
Distance From W12: 206.9 miles
(3 hrs 32 mins)
2017/18 Position: 1st (League One)

Impressively, all three clubs relegated from the Championship in 2016/17 secured an instant return to England's second tier last season. Paul Cook's Wigan were the cream of the League One crop, winning the title with some 98 points in total. The Latics were a Premier League outfit only five years ago – and their brand of free-flowing football under Cook could push them even closer to a return to the big time this season.

STAR MAN
Will Grigg (ST)

2018/19 CHAMPIONSHIP LINE-UP

ASTON VILLA	LEEDS UNITED	READING
BRENTFORD	IPSWICH TOWN	ROTHERHAM UNITED
BOLTON WANDERERS	MIDDLESBROUGH	SHEFFIELD UNITED
BRISTOL CITY	MILLWALL	SHEFFIELD WEDNESDAY
BIRMINGHAM CITY	NORWICH CITY	STOKE CITY
BLACKBURN ROVERS	NOTTINGHAM FOREST	SWANSEA CITY
DERBY COUNTY	PRESTON NORTH END	WEST BROMWICH ALBION
HULL CITY	QUEENS PARK RANGERS	WIGAN ATHLETIC

QPRGAMES

Now it's time to see if you can complete our QPR and football-related Spot The Difference and Wordsearch puzzles! Answers on pages 60-61 - good luck!

SPOT THE DIFFERENCE

Jake Bidwell leads the R's out in the pre-season friendly versus AFC Wimbledon. Can you spot the 10 differences in the pictures of the pre-match handshake, though?

WORDSEARCH

```
W O D N I W R E F S N A R T N F R K M C T W C Z N Y N M
F G M G L R F L M Y M D R A C W O L L E Y R F P P C T M
N W B M F O F F S I D E R U L E K L J C E C R Z O Q F Y
Z D R I B B L I N G X N Q C G R X J P D K E H R T F K M
F R Y F Z V N P Z J F N H K M L Z B A W S T N L F Q K E
R P L F I X T U R E Q K H C D L Z E Q E R E G A N A M D
E S E V R E S E R T T M M I W L H N A E R V W S L M T A
E L A O G N E D L O G H M R L B C S K F M J C C N J A C
K S U B S T I T U T E F H T W L O I L B L W Y I P K C A
I N E C E N T R E S P O T T H N R A M J N X C S F K K K
C T M V F B Z R C K V P C A H T G R G I T R L S R J L Y
K K S C A O X J E K R F V H S R W O A M P G E O Y Q E X
K P D N K W U K K D P U C A F B A T O F M D A R C P K V
K N P U A R N L I C N F L W T L P O H T N T N K E L W L
L N F E G F N A M C L E N C K A R N C C L R S I E A Z R
N R D Q N O G Y C R K R F E C G R L T Z E W H C R Y D B
E E B R R A U L G I R O E E N V I C A L L B E K E E Q F
Q D D M A V L T V G X P F I D N M E M L T C E Y F R T R
U L J F H C D T E O E E S F E N X P Y R S R T X E S J M
A E R Y L L D M Y R L S M S Q T C T B C I R M D R X A M
L I W N N D T E V E E L M R R G R H R L H P T P T E K R
I F V C X U Q W R R M A E A Q N L V E E W A Q M T H J T
S D T L N X L P D N N I T Y T N T H D A L J L T H D L T
E I J R A B S S O R C I T F L L J R Y G A B S L Z L D L
R M Q Z N R Y T P W M F L F Z M R M B U N R M Z E K L W
L H L N Y C T N W E N B K Y L T N T T E I T N K R N N Y
Y J B K R K G G K T M Q Y X Q A M H R F F V F V W V G C
D I N J U R Y T I M E J M M G D H N O I T O M O R P M E
```

Here is a list of 50 footie words. All but one are hidden in the grid, can you work out which is missing?

HE'S MAGIC, YOU KNOW!

AUSSIE INTERNATIONAL **MASSIMO LUONGO** PICKED UP THE 2017/18 QPR SUPPORTERS' PLAYER OF THE YEAR AWARD.

The midfielder, who subsequently travelled with his nation to the 2018 World Cup in Russia, beat Luke Freeman and Alex Smithies – who occupied second and third place respectively – to the gong.

Luongo enjoyed a fine season for the Super Hoops, making 39 appearances in all competitions, scoring six goals and providing three assists.

Meanwhile, the departing **Nedum Onuoha** was named the Ray Jones Players' Player of the Year, as voted for by his team-mates.

Former R's skipper Onuoha made 31 appearances last term at the heart of the Rangers defence, earning him the accolade from his peers.

Paul Smyth won the Daphne Biggs Supporters' Young Player of the Year award.

After making a goalscoring debut against Cardiff City on New Year's Day 2018, Smyth featured regularly – scoring again versus Sheffield Wednesday in April, as well as enjoying a goalscoring debut for the Northern Ireland senior side at home to South Korea in late March.

Smyth beat Darnell Furlong and Ebere Eze to the prize.

Junior Hoops members voted for **Luke Freeman** as their Player of the Year.

Freeman's first full season in the blue and white hoops was largely a positive one, with five goals and 12 assists across his 48 appearances.

Elsewhere, **Josh Scowen**'s wonder strike against Barnsley claimed the Kiyan Prince Goal of the Year crown.

Scowen's peach of a strike against his former club on February 3rd beat Paul Smyth (v Sheffield Wednesday) and Pawel Wszolek (v Fulham) into top spot.

And finally, the **Just For Stan Committee** – consisting of Colin Hale, Sarah Benjafield-Clarke, Paul Finney, Ashley Holding, Adrian Wade and Don Shanks, and who helped facilitate the Stan Bowles Benefit Match last July – won a collective Supporter of the Year award.

ROLL OF HONOUR

SPORTITO SUPPORTERS' PLAYER OF THE YEAR
Massimo Luongo

RAY JONES PLAYERS' PLAYER OF THE YEAR
Nedum Onuoha

DAPHNE BIGGS SUPPORTERS' YOUNG PLAYER OF THE YEAR
Paul Smyth

JUNIOR HOOPS PLAYER OF THE YEAR
Luke Freeman

KIYAN PRINCE GOAL OF THE YEAR
Josh Scowen (v Barnsley)

SUPPORTER OF THE YEAR
Just For Stan Committee

TALK OF THE TERRACE

MASSIMO LUONGO WAS YOUR QPR FANS' PLAYER OF THE YEAR FOR 2017/18. But can you name the previous winners from looking at their randomly-selected pictures? Answers on pages 60-61 – good luck!

1975-76

1976-77

1977-78

1978-79

1979-80

1980-81 & 1985-86

1981-82

1982-83

1983-84

1984-85

1986-87

1987-88, 1988-89 & 1989-90

1990-91

1991-92

1992-93

1993-94

1994-95

1995-96

1996-97

1997-98

1998-99

1999-2000

2000-01

2001-02

2002-03

2003-04 & 2007-08

2004-05

2005-06

2006-07

2008-09

2009-10

2010-11

2011-12 & 2012-13

2013-14 & 2014-15

2015-16

2016-17

2018/19 QPR HOME KIT
AVAILABLE NOW

#QPR181

JAKE BIDWELL

Cult Heroes
★ ★ ★

SIMON
STAINROD

Like Ray Wilkins, former R's striker

Simon Stainrod was another

popular addition to The Forever

R's Club – QPR's ex-players'

association. Simon was inducted

in April 2018.

A big crowd favourite, Stainrod is arguably one of the most-skilful players to have worn the famous number 10 shirt at Loftus Road.

Born in Sheffield on February 1st 1959, he started his career with hometown club Sheffield United before switching to Oldham Athletic. Simon then joined QPR for £270,000 in November 1980.

Stainrod was part of the Rangers team that reached the 1982 FA Cup final under the guidance of Terry Venables, then gained promotion to the top-flight the following season and qualified for the UEFA Cup 12 months later.

In total, he made 177 appearances for the Super Hoops, scoring 62 goals.

"THE FANS ARE VERY SPECIAL AT QPR"

"The fans are very special at QPR," said Stainrod.

"The cup final was a special moment – while the semi-final [versus West Bromwich Albion at neutral Highbury] was even better.

"My number one moment was scoring three goals away at Sheffield Wednesday (November 1981). We won 3-1.

"Terry Venables was the best manager. He could see things in players that others couldn't. And he motivated you to the point where you wanted to do it for him.

"He's the only manager that got that out of me. He was a star."

Stainrod went on to join Sheffield Wednesday in 1985, and also subsequently turned out for Aston Villa, Stoke City, RC Strasbourg, FC Rouen, Falkirk, Dundee and Ayr United. He would later manage both Dundee and Ayr.

Simon has since been based overseas, working in football agency.

PIC OF THE BUNCH
WINNING AWAY!

Our best win on the road last term? Probably the 3-1 victory against promotion chasers Aston Villa at Villa Park.

Goals from Ryan Manning (12 minutes), Jake Bidwell (33) and Luke Freeman (82) put the R's on course for success, with James Chester's 88th minute effort for the hosts proving to be little more than scant consolation.

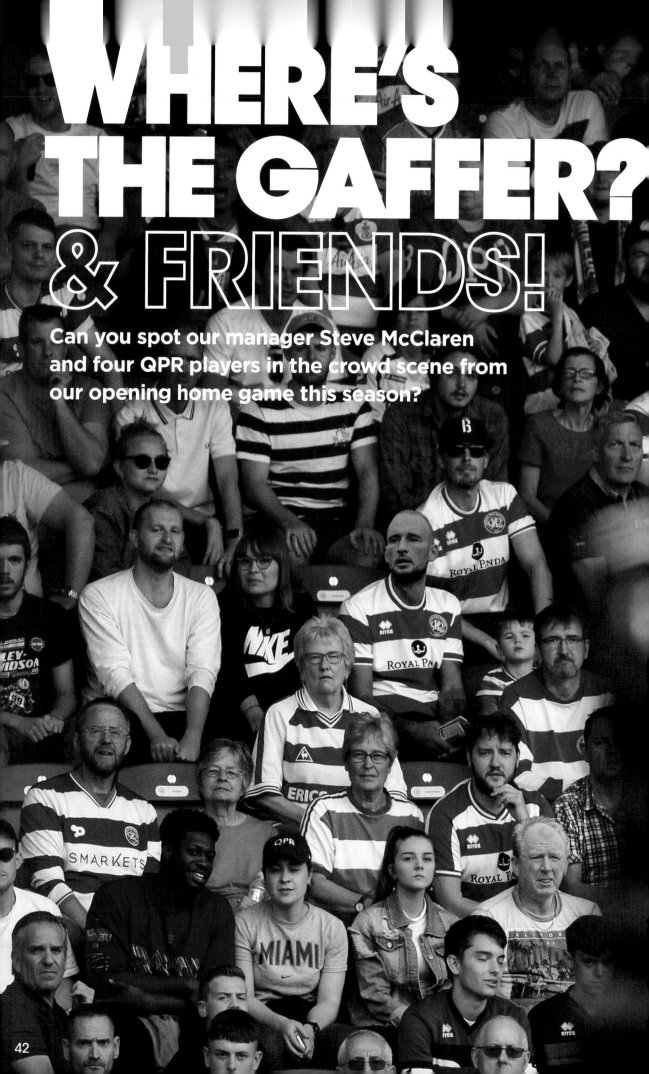

WHERE'S THE GAFFER?
& FRIENDS!

Can you spot our manager Steve McClaren and four QPR players in the crowd scene from our opening home game this season?

MASSIMO LUONGO

PAUL SMYTH

TOP BINS!

PICK that one out!

Midfield enforcer Josh Scowen – who enjoyed an impressive maiden campaign at QPR – was the winner of last year's goal of the season vote, following his long-range stunner against former team Barnsley at Loftus Road in February. It proved to be the only goal of the game, as Rangers ran out 1-0 victors in W12.

KNOW YOUR RANGERS?

THE SEASON OF 2017/18 WAS ANOTHER ACTION-PACKED ONE FOR THE R'S! BUT HOW WELL CAN YOU REMEMBER THE CAMPAIGN THAT WAS?

Test your knowledge by completing our 25-question quiz. Answers on pages 60-61 – good luck!

1 QPR kicked off the campaign with a 2-0 home success over Reading. Whose brace helped us get the better of the Royals?

2 Summer signing Josh Scowen made his league debut for the R's against Reading. Josh arrived at Loftus Road from which fellow Championship outfit?

3 Which former fans' favourite was responsible for taking Ebere Eze on loan for part of the 2017/18 season?

4 In 2017/18, QPR celebrated 100 years since our first season at Loftus Road – but do you know which home shirt colours the R's wore 100 years ago?

5 Who did we beat 1-0 at home in round one of the Carabao Cup (August 8th)?

6 Our first point on the road arrived at Sheffield Wednesday on August 12th. Who scored for the R's in the 1-1 Hillsborough draw?

7 Who netted on their first Rangers start in a 3-2 away defeat to Middlesbrough back in September 2017?

8 How many R's players were shown a red card over the course of the campaign?

9 Which international wore the number 22 shirt last season?

10 The boys from W12 registered impressive back-to-back wins over two table-topping sides in the space of four days back in October 2017. Name the opponents.

11 Can you name the QPR scorers in the impressive 3-1 away win at Aston Villa in March 2018?

12 QPR's biggest Loftus Road crowd in 2017/18 came against which club?

13 There were two red cards for QPR in an away match last season, the R's finishing with nine men. Can you name the opponents?

_____

14 Can you also name the two players who were dismissed?

_____

15 Paul Smyth made an impressive start to his QPR career, coming on and notching the winner against which club on New Year's Day, 2018?

_____

16 Which squad number did whizz-kid Smyth have in his debut season?

_____

17 Joe Lumley made his home league debut against which team in 2017/18?

_____

18 Our club captain bid a sad farewell at the end of the season. Name him.

_____

19 Who top scored for the R's (league)

20 And who had the most assists?

_____

21 Our biggest victory of the campaign was 4-1, which came at home on April 2nd 2018. Who did we face?

_____

22 How many goalkeepers did we use in the Sky Bet Championship during the campaign?

_____

23 Over all competitions, who made the most appearances for us?

_____

24 Where did we finish in the league for 2017/18?

_____

25 How many Championship fixtures

MATT SMITH

25 LEISTNER TONI

ROY WEGERLE

RANGERS fans have always loved a mercurial talent – and Roy Wegerle was just that.

He is fondly remembered for winning ITV's Goal Of The Season award at the end of the 1990/91 campaign, following a stunning solo effort against Leeds United at Elland Road in October 1990.

Wegerle waltzed past four despairing defenders before lashing home from 20 yards – helping QPR to a 3-2 victory against a team who went on to be crowned Division One champions the following season.

South-African born Roy was with us between 1989-92, after moving from Luton Town. He began his professional career with the Tampa Bay Rowdies in the USA, and first moved to England to join Chelsea in 1986.

Wegerle was an extremely-skilful player who wore our coveted number 10 shirt with great distinction.

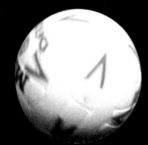

"I WAS ALWAYS AWARE OF THE TRADITION FOR FLAIR PLAYERS"

"I had two-and-a-half lovely years at Loftus Road," he said. It was probably the most-enjoyable time for me during my career in England. Certainly, I played my best football when I was with Rangers.

"I was always aware of the tradition for flair players. After all, it was Rodney Marsh who originally helped me to get to England after my college days in America. Then I heard all the stories about Stan Bowles."

Wegerle made 93 appearances for the Super Hoops and scored 31 goals. He eventually moved on to Blackburn Rovers for £1million in March 1992, before spells at Coventry City and back in the US in Major League Soccer.

Due to his American citizenship, Wegerle represented the States at both the 1994 and 1998 World Cups before retiring from football.

He subsequently became a professional golfer for a short period, and now resides in Miami, Florida.

DERBY DAY HIGHLIGHT

Rangers came from two goals down to draw 2-2 against another promotion-chasing team in near neighbours Fulham at Craven Cottage.

Strikes from Tom Cairney (32 minutes) and Lucas Piazon (45) put the Whites in command – but Rangers replied through Massimo Luongo (45+3) and Paweł Wszołek (81) to spark wild scenes of celebration among Rangers' strong army of travelling supporters!

NUMBERS UP!

QPR confirmed their 2018/19 squad numbers ahead of the new Sky Bet Championship season.

The iconic number 10 shirt is back in use this term – and was handed to R's playmaker Ebere Eze for the campaign. The number was used to pay tribute to the great Stan Bowles in 2017/18.

Meanwhile, following the departure of Alex Smithies to Cardiff City, the number one jersey was allocated to Matt Ingram. Fellow goalkeeper Joe Lumley now wears the number 13 top.

Elsewhere, Joel Lynch has opted to wear the number 33, with Sean Goss taking Lynch's vacant number six shirt.

Diminutive attacker Paul Smyth moved to 38, and new signing Toni Leistner is wearing the 37 shirt he wore at Union Berlin.

Bright Osayi-Samuel (20), Paweł Wszołek (23) and David Wheeler (25) were other notable changes.

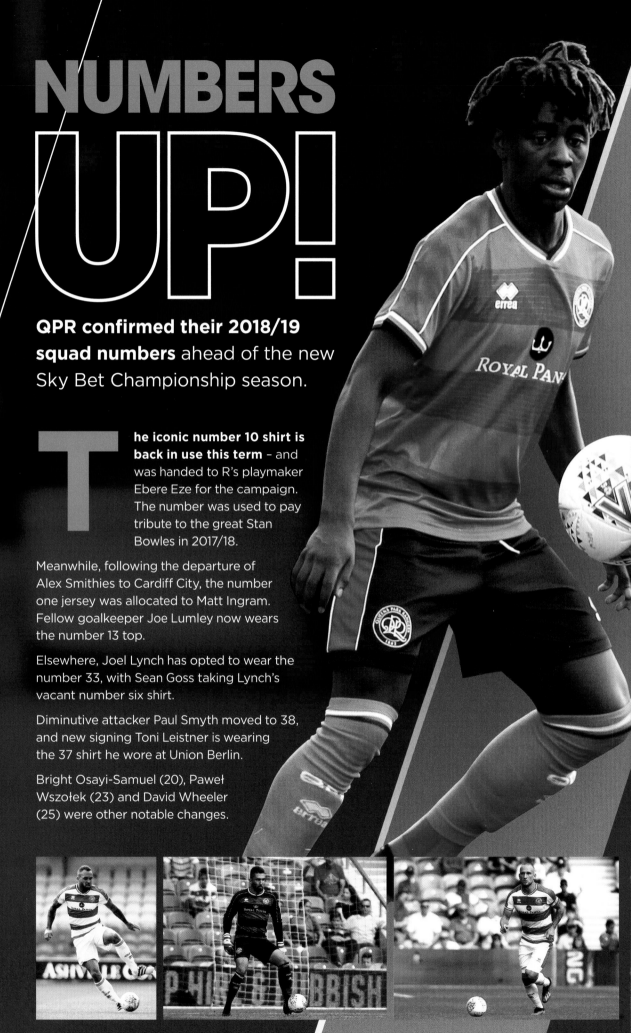

SQUAD NUMBERS

1	MATT INGRAM		27	OLAMIDE SHODIPO
2	DARNELL FURLONG		28	NIKO HAMALAINEN
3	JAKE BIDWELL		29	GILES PHILLIPS
4	GRANT HALL		30	CHARLIE OWENS
6	SEAN GOSS		31	RAY JONES
7	LUKE FREEMAN		33	JOEL LYNCH
8	JORDAN COUSINS		37	TONI LEISTNER
9	CONOR WASHINGTON		38	PAUL SMYTH
10	EBERE EZE		40	IDRISSA SYLLA
11	JOSH SCOWEN			
13	JOE LUMLEY			
14	RYAN MANNING			
15	ALEX BAPTISTE			
17	MATT SMITH			
18	ARAMIDE OTEH			
19	ILIAS CHAIR			
20	BRIGHT OSAYI-SAMUEL			
21	MASSIMO LUONGO			
23	PAWEL WSZOLEK			
24	OSMAN KAKAY			
25	DAVID WHEELER			
26	SENY DIENG			

2018/19 QPR AWAY KIT
AVAILABLE NOW

#QPR1819

OSAYI-SAMUEL

ANSWERS

TALK OF THE TERRACE (P34)

WHERE'S THE GAFFER & FRIENDS (P42)

MATT SMITH

TONI LEISTNER

LUKE FREEMAN

STEVE McCLAREN

MASSIMO LUONGO

1975/76	Phil Parkes
1976/77	David Webb
1977/78	Stan Bowles
1978/79	John Hollins
1979/80	Clive Allen
1980/81 & 1985/86	
Steve Wicks	
1981/82	Tony Currie
1982/83	John Gregory
1983/84	Peter Hucker
1984/85	Terry Fenwick
1986/87	Alan McDonald
1987/88, 1988/89 &	
1989/90	Paul Parker
1990/91	Roy Wegerle
1991/92	Clive Wilson
1992/93	Les Ferdinand
1993/94	David Bardsley
1994/95	Andrew Impey
1995/96	Trevor Sinclair

1996/97	John Spencer	2006/07	Lee Cook
1997/98	Karl Ready	2008/09	
1998/99	Danny Maddix	Damion Stewart	
1999/2000		2009/10	
Stuart Wardley		Alejandro Faurlin	
2000/01	Peter Crouch	2010/11	Paddy Kenny
2001/02	Terrell Forbes	2011/12 & 2012/13	
2002/03	Kevin Gallen	Clint Hill	
2003/04 & 2007/08		2013/14 & 2014/15	
Martin Rowlands		Charlie Austin	
2004/05	Paul Furlong	2015/16	Grant Hall
2005/06	Danny Shittu	2016/17	Alex Smithies

QUIZ (P48)

1. Conor Washington
2. Barnsley
3. Gareth Ainsworth (Wycombe Wanderers)
4. Green & White Hoops
5. Northampton Town
6. Jamie Mackie
7. David Wheeler
8. 5
9. Paweł Wszołek
10. Wolves & Sheffield United
11. Ryan Manning, Jake Bidwell, Luke Freeman
12. Aston Villa (16,934)
13. Preston North End
14. Alex Baptiste & Jamie Macki
15. Cardiff City
16. 37
17. Birmingham City
18. Nedum Onuoha
19. Matt Smith (11)
20. Luke Freeman (12)
21. Norwich City
22. 3 (Alex Smithies, Matt Ingra Joe Lumley)
23. Luke Freeman (48)
24. 16th
25. 15

WORDSEARCH (P31)

```
W O D N I W R E F S N A R T N F R K M C T W C Z N Y N M
F G M G L R F L M Y M D R A C W O L L E Y R F P P C T M
N W B M F O F F S I D E R U L E K L J C E C R Z O Q F Y
Z D R I B B L I N G X N Q C G R X J P D K E H R T F K M
F R Y F Z V N P Z J F N H K M L Z B A W S T N L F Q K E
R P L F I X T U R E Q K H C D L Z E Q E R E G A N A M D
E S E V R E S E R T T M M I W L H N A E R V W S L M T A
K L A O G N E D L O G H M R L B C S K F M J C C N J A C
I N E C E N T R E S P O T T H N R A M J N X C S F K K K
C T M V F B Z R C K V P C A H T G R G I T R L S R J L Y
K K S C A O X J E K R F V H S R W O A M P G E O Y Q E X
K P D N K W U K K D P U C A F B A T O F M D A R C P K V
K N P U A R N L I C N F L W T L P O H T N T N K E L W L
L N F E G F N A M C L E N C K A R N C C L R S I E A Z R
N R D Q N O G Y C R K R F E C G R L T Z E W H C R Y D B
E E B R R A U L G I R O E N V I C A L L B E K E E Q F
Q D D M A V L T V G X P F I D N M E M L T C E Y F R T R
U L J F H C D T E O E S F E N X P Y R S R T X E S J M
A E R Y L L D M Y R L S M S Q T C T B C I R M D R X A M
L I W N N D T E V E E L M R R G R H R L H P T P T E K R
I F V C X U Q W R R M A E A Q N L V E E W A Q M T H J T
S D T L N X L P D N N I T Y T N T H D A L J L T H D L T
E I J R A B S S O R C I T F L L J R Y G A B S L Z L D L
R M Q Z N R Y T P W M F L F Z M R M B U N R M Z X K L W
L H L N Y C T N W E N B K Y L T N T T E I T N K R N N Y
Y J B K R K G G K T M Q Y X Q A M H R F F V F V W V G C
D I N J U R Y T I M E J M M G D H N O I T O M O R P M E
```

FIXTURES 2018/19

2018

AUGUST

4th August 3:00 PM
Preston North End (A)
Sky Bet Championship

11th August 3:00 PM
Sheffield United (H)
Sky Bet Championship

18th August 3:00 PM
West Bromwich Albion (A)
Sky Bet Championship

21st August 7:45 PM
Bristol City (H)
Sky Bet Championship

25th August 3:00 PM
Wigan Athletic (H)
Sky Bet Championship

SEPTEMBER

1st September 3:00 PM
Birmingham City (A)
Sky Bet Championship

15th September 3:00 PM
Bolton Wanderers (A)
Sky Bet Championship

19th September 7:45 PM
Millwall (H)
Sky Bet Championship

22nd September 5:30 PM
Norwich City (H)
Sky Bet Championship

29th September 3:00 PM
Swansea City (A)
Sky Bet Championship

OCTOBER

2nd October 8:00 PM
Reading (A)
Sky Bet Championship

6th October 3:00 PM
Derby County (H)
Sky Bet Championship

20th October 3:00 PM
Ipswich Town (A)
Sky Bet Championship

23rd October 7:45 PM
Sheffield Wednesday (H)
Sky Bet Championship

27th October 3:00 PM
Aston Villa (H)
Sky Bet Championship

NOVEMBER

3rd November 3:00 PM
Blackburn Rovers (A)
Sky Bet Championship

10th November 3:00 PM
Brentford (H)
Sky Bet Championship

24th November 3:00 PM
Stoke City (A)
Sky Bet Championship

27th November 7:45 PM
Rotherham United (A)
Sky Bet Championship

DECEMBER

1st December 3:00 PM
Hull City (H)
Sky Bet Championship

8th December 3:00 PM
Leeds United (A)
Sky Bet Championship

15th December 3:00 PM
Middlesbrough (H)
Sky Bet Championship

22nd December 3:00 PM
Nottingham Forest (A)
Sky Bet Championship